Harold's Dog
Horace Is Scared
of the Dark

Elizabeth R. Skoglund
Pictures by Dale Bjorkman

Tyndale House
Publishers, Inc.
Wheaton, Illinois

Philippians 3:13-14 text is from *New Testament in Modern Speech* by
R. F. Weymouth, D.Lit. (Grand Rapids, Mich.: Kregel, 1978). Philippians
4:6 text is from *Notes on the Epistles of Saint Paul* by J. D. Lightfoot.
Philippians 4:8 text and Psalm 139:5 text are from *The Living Bible,*
© 1971 owned by assignment by KNT Charitable Trust. All rights
reserved.

Library of Congress Cataloging-in-Publication Data

Skoglund, Elizabeth.
    Harold's dog Horace is scared of the dark / Elizabeth R. Skoglund.
      p. cm.—(I can talk about it) (Eager reader)
    Summary: Harold and his dog Horace discover that their fear of the
dark, and other bad thoughts, can be banished by thinking about God.
    ISBN 0-8423-1047-9
    [1. Fear of the dark—Fiction. 2. Bedtime—Fiction. 3. Christian
life—Fiction. 4. Dogs—Fiction.] I. Title. II. Series.
III. Series: Eager reader.
PZ7.S628353Har 1992
[E]—dc20   92-3597

Printed in the United States of America
98 97 96 95 94 93 92
8 7 6 5 4 3 2 1

To the memory of G. L. Harrington, M.D.

It was late Friday afternoon. Harold and Horace arrived at Aunt Louise and Uncle Dave's beach cottage. They came to spend the weekend.

"Aunt Louise!" Harold said excitedly as the door opened. "Look at my new tape recorder. Now I can listen to songs whenever I want to. I can hear my favorite stories, too. I can't wait to show you how it works."

Aunt Louise gave Harold a big hug.
She gave Horace a pat on the head.
Horace wagged his tail and rolled over.

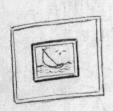  

Aunt Louise took Harold to a small
bedroom at the back of the cottage. It
had a big window with white, fluffy
curtains. The window looked out on the
ocean. Harold looked out of the open
window. Horace looked, too. Harold
saw some men fishing from a small boat.

Aunt Louise helped Harold put his
things away.

Then Harold and Horace followed
Aunt Louise to the kitchen. Harold sat
down. Horace sat too. Aunt Louise had
just finished making a batch of peanut
brittle. She gave Harold a great big
piece.

Horace sat very still. He stared hard
at the peanut brittle. He nudged
Harold's knee. He barked one short bark.

"*Shhh!*" Harold said. But then he
gave Horace a piece.

"My tape recorder is easy to use,"
Harold explained to Aunt Louise.
"When you push PLAY, the tape plays.
Then when you want to stop it, you
press STOP. You can hear anything you
want."

Harold played a Bible story about a
man named Daniel. It told how Daniel
was thrown into a big den of lions.

Suddenly, Harold pushed STOP. "Sometimes this story scares Horace," he explained. "It might scare you too."

Then Harold put in another tape. He pushed PLAY. "Jesus Loves the Little Children" started playing.

"I like that song," Harold said happily.

Just then Uncle Dave came through the door. Horace barked a happy bark. Harold ran to greet him.

Uncle Dave had two fishing poles in his hand. "Guess what?" said Uncle Dave. "Tomorrow you, Horace, and I are going fishing."

"Oh boy!" said Harold. "I was hoping you'd say that."

After dinner Uncle Dave started a big
fire in the fireplace. Harold and Horace
lay down in front of the fire. Outside,
the wind started to blow. It blew hard.
The waves from the sea crashed noisily
against the beach. It was almost time to
go to bed.

Aunt Louise filled the big tub with
water. Harold took his toy submarine off
of the bathroom shelf and stepped into
the warm water.

Then Harold heard the deep, sad sound of a foghorn. A foghorn warns ships that they are near the shore. Its sound stops ships from crashing on the rocks. Harold thought about ships crashing. He shivered. The submarine sank to the bottom of the tub.

Harold got out of the tub. He dried himself quickly and got into his pajamas. Then he ran to his bedroom.

Uncle Dave came into the room just
as Harold was climbing into bed.

"Horace is afraid of the dark,"
Harold said.

Uncle Dave gave Horace a hug.
"Why is Horace afraid?" he asked.

"Well," said Harold slowly. "He's
afraid someone will come in and steal
him. He's afraid of funny noises. He's
afraid of big shadows, too."

"Don't worry," said Uncle Dave.
"Horace will have a night-light tonight.
It looks like a brown teddy bear."

The wind shook the bedroom
window. Horace started to shake.
Harold became very quiet.

After Uncle Dave left, Harold snuggled
down under the large patchwork quilt.
Horace curled up on the rug by the bed.
Over in the corner a small brown bear
glowed in the dark. But in the darkness
he began to look mean.

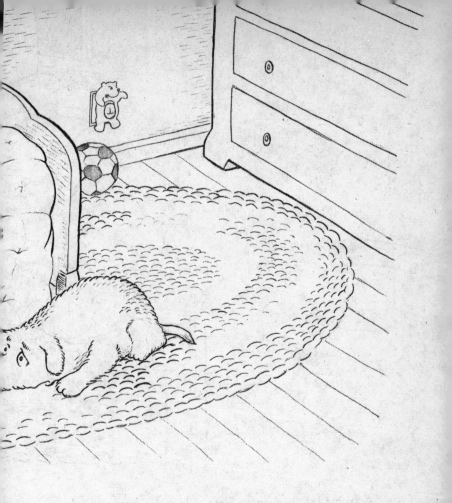

The wind wailed. The window rattled. The waves crashed against the shore. A branch scratched against the windowpane. Now the foghorn sounded like an angry, wounded animal.

Suddenly Harold sat straight up in bed. Horace jumped up on top of Harold. Horace was shaking.

"Aunt Louise! Uncle Dave!" Harold shouted. "Horace is still afraid of the dark!"

A few minutes later, Harold and
Horace were curled up on the couch in
front of the fireplace. Aunt Louise
brought in three cups of steaming hot
chocolate. Each cup had marshmallows on
top! Uncle Dave stirred up the fire.

The wind didn't seem as wild anymore.
The foghorn sounded more like a friendly
owl saying, "Who?" or "Hello."

"I have an idea," said Aunt Louise.
Aunt Louise always had good ideas
when things got scary.
"What's that?" asked Harold.
Horace sniffed the hot chocolate.

"Well," said Aunt Louise, "sometimes you have happy thoughts. Right?"

"Yes," answered Harold cautiously.

"Let's call them your happy tapes," said Aunt Louise. "They are like the songs and stories you play on your new tape recorder. Your head is like a library of tapes. Can you name some happy tapes that you carry around in your head?"

"I think so," said Harold with a grin. "Coming here to see you is a happy tape. Going fishing with Uncle Dave is a happy tape, too."

"That's good," said Aunt Louise. She put down her cup. "Can you think of others?"

Harold wrinkled his nose. He thought hard. A log fell off the grate in the fireplace. Another branch hit the window. Horace shook. He jumped right into Harold's lap.

"The Bible is full of happy tapes," said Aunt Louise helpfully.

"God loves me," said Harold. "That's a happy tape. God never leaves me is one, too."

Harold drank the rest of his hot chocolate. A big marshmallow floated into his mouth.

"I have another idea," said Harold excitedly. "I can pretend I have a giant tape recorder. I just have to push the pretend PLAY button. Then I can play any of the happy tapes I carry around in my head."

"You can learn more about God's promises," Aunt Louise suggested. "Then you'll have even more happy tapes."

What are some of GODs promises?

food, clothing, sunlight, parents, shelther, Holy Bible, pets, and Jesus.

"Even a song can be a happy tape," said Aunt Louise. "You can sing in bed at night. But you must sing ever so softly."

What are my favorite SONGS?

Don't Stop. I saw the sign. and Jesus loves me.

Suddenly Harold looked confused.
"What about bad tapes?" he asked.
"What about being afraid of the dark?"

"That's easy," answered Aunt Louise. "You can just push your pretend STOP button. You can say stop to the bad tape. And before another bad tape sneaks in, you can push your pretend PLAY button for a happy tape. STOP, PLAY, STOP, PLAY! That's how you handle the tapes you play in your mind."

"Why don't you name some other bad tapes. That way you'll know what tapes to say stop to," said Uncle Dave.

"OK," Harold said. "What if my parents start yelling? What if Grandpa dies? What if my friends call me 'Freckles'? What if I never grow tall?"

Topes to say stop to.

When I try to lie, car axident, lose of job and sins,

"Of course, having freckles and not growing tall aren't really so important, are they?" said Harold.

"Not too important," agreed Uncle Dave.

"But they're important to you," said Aunt Louise. She hugged Harold. "And remember! Your friends will still call you 'Freckles' sometimes. And someday—maybe a long time from now—Grandpa will die. But you don't have to worry about that now. You can push STOP! You can play a happy tape instead."

Harold began to nod his head sleepily. Horace stretched a long stretch.

Aunt Louise tucked Harold back into bed.

Harold scrunched down under the big quilt. Then a streak of lightning shot by the window. Harold grabbed Horace. Horace hid his head under Harold's pillow and started to shake. Quickly Harold pushed his pretend STOP button. He remembered that God has promised, "I will never leave you." He pushed the PLAY button by thanking God for being with him.

Horace peeked out from under the pillow.

"I'm glad you're not afraid of the dark anymore, Horace," Harold said sleepily. "Neither am I."

The next thing Harold knew, it was morning. Horace was licking his face. The sun was shining brightly. It was a perfect day to go fishing.

A Word to Parents

Eight-year-old Tommy was brought to my counseling office after an earthquake had caused some damage to his house while he and his family were inside. As he sat there, nervously telling me how afraid he was of "The Big One," the creaky old elevator outside my office door came down with a shake and a thud. Tommy jumped up with a look of sheer terror. "It's an earthquake!" he shouted.

"It's just the elevator!" I shouted back.

Tommy relaxed into his chair, muttering, "What if we have another earthquake?"

"What if we have another earthquake" is an old tape. When the earthquake occurred, Tommy was justifiably afraid. His fear was an appropriate, normal reaction to an earthquake. And he needed to express his fear. But Tommy turned the normal feeling of fear into an ongoing tape that he played with regularity: *What if we have another earthquake right now?* Unusual noises, a television program mentioning earthquakes, the vibration from a passing truck—all these could trigger the tape. The whole world had become a giant earthquake. Tommy was tormented by this negative tape.

We all have mental tapes. All of us, adults and children alike, carry around in our mind a personal library of old tapes. Some of these tapes are negative and are prefaced by phrases like *What if, Maybe I should have, and Why can't I.* Other tapes consist of memories of a childhood punishment that wasn't fair, the death of a loved one, or betrayal by a trusted friend. Long after the event has passed, we play our tapes of regret and guilt until the event begins to feel as if it just happened all over again. In reality, it is merely a ghost in the cemetery, but we give it flesh.

Some tapes, however, are happy. Dreams of a future career, pleasant memories from childhood, and promises of enablement and blessing from God are just a few examples. These tapes, when played, encourage us and help us stop the negative tapes. The need to have a mental library full of positive tapes is one reason why it is so important to build memories for children. This can be done by taking them to special places, like a children's museum or the birthplace of a parent; by reading to them from various types of books, both fiction and nonfiction; and by celebrating important times like birthdays and Christmas, or even an achievement like an *A* in math or a home run in baseball.

There is an important difference between emotions and mental tapes. Grief, joy, anger, and other emotions need to be expressed in some constructive way and should not be confused with tapes. Tapes, on the other hand, often follow an emotion and can keep it going or re-create it full force. For example, after a death there is grief. Anger, tender reminiscences, and

When I had surgery last year, Psalm 139:5 in *The Living Bible* became my focus: "You both precede and follow me and place your hand of blessing on my head." Whenever a *what if* fear began to play, I stopped that tape and focused on this verse. Of course I was afraid, and I expressed that emotion of fear. But the fear didn't work its way into a negative tape. I didn't dwell on all the negative possibilities. And way down inside I had a sense of God's control over my life. How everything turned out was up to him.

We need to teach children early on how to handle mental tapes. Negative tapes play a major role in the problems that people present in a counseling office like mine, and I see people from age three on up. From simple self-doubt at social events or fear of failure at school, to sheer torment over flying in an airplane, how we handle the tapes in our mental library will determine much of our happiness and effectiveness in this world.

If children can learn to deal with their tapes early in life, it will be a great lesson in mental health. The "let's pretend" game of the giant tape recorder is one way to help achieve this end. Using this image rather than pretending to cut a tape with giant scissors, for example, insures that children realize the tape is not destroyed; it is still there to come back again, but it can be controlled. Since children are used to the world of fantasy, using the pretend method is a simple tool to

p them understand the concept of mental tapes
nore completely.

A child who had lost her mother at Christmas grew disinterested in the festivities when Christmas came the next year. Wandering off from the other children at a party, Melissa confided her feelings to a friend: "I miss my mother. Do you think she's really in heaven? What if I never see her again?"

After some reassurance, Melissa stopped the negative tape and said, "I'm not going to think about this anymore. I'm just going to remember that this year my mother is with Jesus on his birthday." Then came the action that reinforced the new tape: "Let's go and open our Christmas presents!"

Melissa and her friend went back and joined the other children.

Ask your bookstore for other Eager Reader books:

Alfred MacDuff Is Afraid of War
Corey's Dad Drinks Too Much
I Want a Puppy!
Stranger Danger
Natalie Jean and the Flying Machine
Natalie Jean Goes Hog Wild
Natalie Jean and Tag-along Tessa
Natalie Jean and the Haints' Parade
Three Cheers for Big Ears